DISCOVERING
THE EMPIRE
OF GHANA

ROBERT Z. COHEN

ROSEN
PUBLISHING®

New York

Published in 2014 by The Rosen Publishing Group, Inc.
29 East 21st Street, New York, NY 10010

Library of Congress Cataloging-in-Publication Data

Cohen, Robert Z., author.
Discovering the empire of Ghana/Robert Z. Cohen. — First edition.
    pages cm. — (Exploring African civilizations)
ISBN 978-1-4777-1882-7 (library binding)
1. Ghana (Empire)—History—Juvenile literature. 2. Ghana (Empire)—Kings and rulers—Juvenile literature. 3. Ghana (Empire)—Civilization—Juvenile literature.
I. Title. II. Series: Exploring African civilizations.
DT532.15.C64 2014
966.1016—dc23

                                                                    2013023156

Manufactured in the United States of America

CPSIA Compliance Information: Batch #W14YA: For further information, contact Rosen Publishing, New York, New York, at 1-800-237-9932.

A portion of the material in this book has been derived from *The Empire of Ghana* by Rebecca L. Green.

CONTENTS

INTRODUCTION

The meeting of Europe and Africa began on the dry grasslands of West Africa well over one thousand years ago. Europe and the Middle East hungered for gold. Africa south of the Sahara Desert had gold. The powerful kings of the Empire of Ghana controlled the gold trade.

Ghana was the first of a series of West African empires that grew along the dry southern shores of the Sahara Desert. Think of the Sahara as a vast sea of sand. Along the southern rim of this sea of sand are grasslands and port cities, where camel caravans serve as transportation instead of boats and where people from different nations and cultures meet for the first time. This area is known as the Sahel. It may look dry and dusty, but it holds immeasurable wealth. Not only goods are exchanged, but ideas as well.

Ghana's reputation led medieval mapmakers and even Africans to refer to all of West Africa as "Ghana" or "Guinea." In Moroccan Arabic, it was known as *Gnawa*. Among Africans taken to the New World as slaves, it was remembered in the Haitian Creole language as *Giné*, the land to which slaves' souls would fly when they died.

The first written records of West African history come from early Arab sources who called the region south of the Sahara desert *Bilad al-Sudan*, or "Land of the Black People." (The modern African nations known as Sudan and the new South Sudan are, in fact, on the eastern side of the Sahara.) The kingdom of Ghana was located just south of the great Sahara Desert, between the Niger River and the Senegal River in a region

The sun rises over the Senegal River. Medieval traders who traveled to the Empire of Ghana nicknamed it the "River of Gold."

called Wangara. This area lies in the countries now called Mali, Mauritania, Niger, Burkina Faso, Gambia, and Senegal.

The vast Sahara Desert had served as a barrier between Western civilization and sub-Saharan Africa. The power and wealth of the king of the Ghana Empire, however, was too great to keep secret for long. In the dry grasslands, the cultures of Africa and the West first met, traded, and clashed.

The reputation of the Empire of Ghana has led to many confusing labels. The Empire of Ghana is not related to the modern African country known today as Ghana, which adopted the name of the ancient empire in 1957 upon gaining independence from the British Empire. The modern country of Ghana is located on the coast, bordering the Atlantic Ocean.

It is not known when ancient Ghana was founded, although it may have been as early as 250 CE. We do know that it developed into a wealthy trading empire that flourished from about 750 until 1076 CE. For years, scholars had little real evidence of this fabled kingdom and did not know if it was real or simply a product of legends and travelers' tales. That changed with the translation of an ancient Arabic book from the library of the city of Timbuktu in Mali. The text led to the discovery of the remains of the ancient capital city, Kumbi Saleh, in 1914. The empire of legend is now a part of history.

CHAPTER ONE

The Soninke: From Wagadou to Ghana

The Empire of Ghana, also called Wagadou, was the first of several African kingdoms that had flourished in the grasslands bordering the southern rim of the Sahara Desert. This area is known as the Sahel, an Arabic word that means "the shore."

Several major rivers cross the western Sahel. These would flood each year, making farming and fishing possible along the banks. The main rivers in the area are the Senegal River, the Gambia River, and most important, the long Niger River, which flows to the east. Along these rivers, ancient nomadic African peoples developed a new sedentary (settled) way of life.

In addition to irrigation, the rivers provided water, fish, and transportation. Hunters settled down to farm, and farming led to village life. To maintain a settled village life, people needed iron tools to break the hard ground for planting. This led to the development of mining, metalworking, and trade among the different peoples living along the rivers.

Around the time that the Roman Empire flourished in Europe, a chief of the Soninke people established an alliance of similar people into a kingdom. They were united under the central rule of this king, who was called the *ghana* in the

The Empire of Ghana extended its influence through trade along the rivers of the Sahel region, including the Senegal, Niger, and Gambia rivers.

Soninke language. It would eventually grow into the strongest and richest empire in sub-Saharan Africa by the fourth century CE.

The Origin Myth of Dinga

Many cultures depend on oral histories instead of written books to remember the past. In West Africa, oral histories are studied and constantly retold by professional historians—musicians called griots. Oral histories about the origin of the Empire of Ghana begin with a story of the first Soninke ancestor, Dinga.

According to legend, Dinga came from the east and traveled a long time to reach the place that would become Ghana. When Dinga and his family finally settled, they established a group of communities, each headed by one of Dinga's sons. These communities prospered and grew into the first kingdom of the ancient Soninke.

The Soninke people were divided into clans. A clan is a group

Griots are singers whose ballads preserve the history of West African peoples. Many play the *kora*, a harp built out of a large, dry gourd.

of families that all descend from one common ancestor. Each clan performed a different job. For example, members of the Kante clan were blacksmiths and metalworkers. Members of the royal family were all from the Cissé clan. These great family lines still exist today.

The Wagadou State

The Soninke people who lived in ancient Ghana called themselves the Wago people and called their kingdom Wagadou. It was only later that Wagadou came to be known by the name Ghana, which is the Mande word for "war chief." When Arabic writers wrote about the kingdom, they called it *Bilad Ghana*, which means "the country (*bilad*) of the king (*ghana*)" of the Soninke people. Eventually, the phrase was shortened to "Ghana."

The first known king of Wagadou was Kaya Magan Cissé, who lived around 350 CE. He founded the Cissé Tounkara royal family, which would go on to dominate the Empire of Ghana to the eighth century CE. Even after the decline of Ghana, the Cissé family continued to be a strong presence in the history of African kingdoms of the Sahel.

The term "ghana" emphasizes one of the king's important roles—that of military leader. The Soninke had a particularly fearsome military force because of their skill in working iron to make tools and weapons. Metal tools also made farming more productive. This meant that a few people could grow enough food for the entire population, which allowed the population to increase in size. This allowed Wagadou to maintain large

THE MANDE PEOPLES

Today, the area once occupied by the Empire of Ghana is home to several different ethnic groups. Many belong to a larger group known as the Mande people, who speak versions of the Mande languages, which are among the most widespread languages in West Africa today. Between Senegal in the west, Mauritania in the north, Guinea and Cote D'Ivoire in the south, and Nigeria in the east, one

Mande houses are built from mud and reed thatch. They are easy to build and repair, and they provide a cool escape from the Saharan heat.

can find speakers of many forms of the Mande language family: Mandinka, Malinke, Bambara, Dioula, and Soninke. The kings of Ghana were Soninke, whose dialect is quite distinct from Mandinka. The Soninke were also known as the Sarakole.

Other ethnic groups speaking different languages also lived in the western Sahel region. The Fulani (also known as Peul or Fulbe) were nomads herding sheep and goats. Along the Niger River to the east were farming people who spoke the Songhay language. The neighboring Serer people were the first West African people to build cities and adapt to an urban way of life.

North of the Ghana Empire lived people known as Berbers and, after the spread of Islam across North Africa in the eighth century, Arabs. The clash of cultures and religions between these people and the Soninke kings would eventually signal the end of Ghana's power and influence.

In the era of the transatlantic slave trade, many Mande people were among the Africans sold into slavery in the New World, particularly to North America, where they became known as "Mandingos." Many African American folk and religious traditions, such as stories, recipes, and even musical styles, can be traced back to a strong Mande heritage.

professional armies. Wagadou soldiers equipped with metal swords and spears could easily defeat rivals who fought with wooden weapons.

The Wagadou kingdom absorbed many of the peoples it conquered. Some of the defeated peoples were allowed to continue living under the authority of their own rulers. But they had to pledge allegiance to the Wagadou kings and pay tribute, or taxes, to them.

Controlling a Vast Empire

At the height of its power, Wagadou stretched from the Atlantic Ocean in the west to the southern bend of the Niger River in the east. It expanded beyond present-day Mali and Mauritania into what are now the countries of Senegal and Guinea.

At this time, the only way for a king to communicate with people in other parts of the kingdom was to send a messenger by horseback, and this could take many days. It was an inefficient way to run a large country. To overcome this problem, the Wagadou kings divided ancient Ghana into provinces and appointed princes to rule over them. Although the princes were rulers of their own provinces, they obeyed the central king in the city of Kumbi Saleh and paid taxes to him. This system of government was similar to the European feudal system. It gave the king ultimate control over a much larger area.

A Wagadou ruler had many roles in addition to being the military leader. The Soninke considered their kings divine, or godlike. Whenever the king appeared, the people fell to the ground and threw dirt on their heads as a sign of humility and respect for the king, who was believed to represent the soul of the entire population.

This combination of roles made the Wagadou king extremely powerful. The Soninke were matrilineal, which means that power and identity were passed down through the women of the family. Therefore, when a king died, he was not succeeded by his son but by his nephew—his sister's son. Although the Wagadou rulers were men, women held very important positions. Matrilineal societies—in which power, descent, and inheritance are determined by the woman's side of the family—are still widespread in West Africa.

CHAPTER TWO

The Power of Trade

As the Wagadou kingdom grew and matured, it became more and more powerful. The kingship system created stability and peace. This meant that the people of the empire could cultivate their land without fear of war. They grew many crops, such as cotton and the grains millet and sorghum. As these crops prospered, the king's subjects had enough food to eat and a surplus of food to sell to others. This led to a wide trade network.

The Land of Gold

As trade flourished in Wagadou, the Soninke began to trade gold. While early Wagadou kings were called "ghana" because of their military prowess, later kings were called *kaya maghan*, which means "master" or "king of the gold."

The regions surrounding ancient Ghana contained a great variety of natural resources. The two most important were salt and gold. Salt is essential to human life, while gold is a luxury. Today, because salt is easily available, we tend to forget that it is vital for human survival. To people living in areas without it, salt was worth its weight in gold.

The Wagadou kingdom was in the perfect position to profit from all of this trade. Its strategic location along West African trade routes allowed its rulers to become very wealthy and powerful. Northern merchants living in the desert oases who wanted to travel to the southern forests to sell their surplus goods—including salt from Teghaza in the desert and metal tools—had to pass through the kingdom. Southern merchants traveled north to sell their gold, ivory, and slaves.

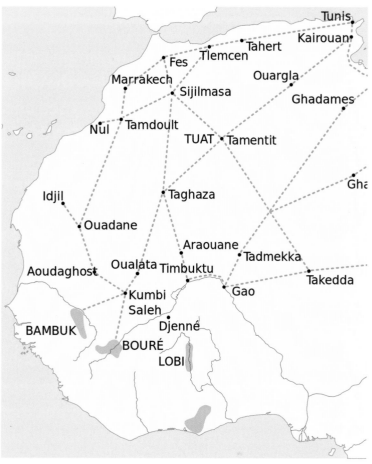

The city of Kumbi Saleh was well placed to take advantage of the trans-Saharan trade in gold, salt, and slaves.

The Burden of Taxes

The kings of Wagadou were able to profit from the transport and sale of these important and expensive goods. They demanded that traders and their caravans pay a tax each time they entered and left the kingdom. For example, northern traders had to pay one measure of gold to the king for each container of salt they brought into the kingdom. Southern

THE SAHARA DESERT

The Sahara Desert is the single largest hot desert in the world, stretching across North Africa from the Atlantic Ocean in the west to the Red Sea and Indian Ocean in the east, taking up at least one-tenth of the entire African continent. Its name comes from the Arabic word for "great desert." While it is one of the most hostile environments on Earth for people to live in, it has been inhabited since the Stone Age. Although the Sahara is mostly dry and rocky, there are also areas with spring-fed water known as oases (singular: oasis), where people can live and farm.

The Sahara has gone through periods in history in which it was much wetter and cooler than it is today. Throughout the desert, there are hundreds of Stone Age rock paintings called petroglyphs that show early nomadic people hunting animals. This is evidence that the region once had a milder climate.

Archaeologists have also uncovered clay cooking pots. These show that the ancient Saharan people cooked porridge and fish stews and lived in settled communities. Around 3900 BCE, however, the Sahara began to dry out. This caused people to flee to the valleys of larger rivers to maintain their settled farming lifestyles. In the east, this led to the Nubian—and eventually, the Egyptian—civilizations along the Nile River. In the west, the Mandinka cultures responded to their environment in a similar manner, settling in farming groups along the Niger, Gambia, and Senegal rivers.

As the desert grew drier, it proved to be a barrier that few people crossed until the arrival of the domestic camel from the Arabian Peninsula around 200 CE. The camel was the perfect solution to Saharan travel and trade. The camel's body evolved to use water as efficiently as possible. Its fat is stored in its hump, rather than spread evenly around its body. This allows it to stay cooler in hot environments, and the water stored in this fat allows the animal to go for many days without drinking.

The Berber people known as Tuaregs became masters of the camel. They controlled the camel caravans that moved trade goods across the Sahara, stopping at hidden oasis springs to water their camels along the way. A caravan could easily number over a thousand camels. Camel caravans led by Tuaregs continue to be used to carry trade goods across the Sahara to this day.

The arrival of the domestic camel from Arabia connected the African Sahel and the Mediterranean world through a web of caravan routes.

traders had to pay two measures of gold as they carried the same containers out of the kingdom. As a result, traders had to pay taxes twice on the same merchandise: on their way to the market to sell and on their way home after buying or trading.

The gold from these taxes went to the Wagadou king. The king used this money to maintain the Wagadou army and the government, both of which kept the country at peace and trading conditions stable. As the kingdom's power and influence grew in the region, it became large enough to be regarded as an empire—the Empire of Ghana.

The Silent Trade

Many people knew the name of the place where gold was mined: Wangara. But few people knew where Wangara was because trade did not take place at the mines. In fact, foreign traders never met the Wangara traders face-to-face. This protected the gold by keeping secret the location of the gold mines and the identity of the miners.

Instead, traders conducted a "silent trade" in which Soninke middlemen led foreign traders to a selected site. There, the traders unloaded their merchandise—especially salt—onto the ground, beat a large drum to announce their arrival, and left. The Wangara traders then came and placed gold next to the merchandise left by the foreign traders. Then they, too, left. The foreign traders returned. If they were satisfied that the amount of gold left by the Wangara traders was a fair exchange for the goods that they had brought, they took the gold, beat the drum to mark the end of the trade, and left. If they were not satisfied, they left without taking the gold or beating the drum and waited for the Wangara traders to add more gold (if they agreed to do so).

Just as it is today, gold was a luxury item in the ancient Empire of Ghana. The kings carefully controlled the amount of gold leaving the southern mines to ensure that the market never became flooded with gold. They knew that if gold was common and easy to get, it would no longer be a special object, and its price would fall.

The kings controlled the flow of gold by making rules about who could own it. They kept the gold nuggets for themselves and allowed the merchants to trade only in gold dust. The traders and other people obeyed the kings because they believed that only the king was powerful enough to handle gold nuggets. He could do so because he was divine, but it was thought too dangerous for ordinary people to keep gold nuggets themselves.

The Wagadou kings made sure that gold's value did not decrease and that the gold supply did not run out. In fact, they continued to control the gold supply long after Europe's gold mines began to run dry. Rulers of other African, European, and Muslim kingdoms had to travel to the Empire of Ghana (or meet with merchants trading with Ghana and paying taxes to Ghana) for the gold they required to create their coins and regalia.

The Wagadou kings were constantly challenged by their neighbors, who also wished to profit from the gold trade. One of the Soninke people's main rivals was the Berber people to

Until the European discovery of the New World in 1492, West Africa was the source of most of the raw gold traded in Europe and the Arab world.

the north, who continually tried to capture some of the empire's gold mines. Finally, in about 990 CE, the Wagadou king took advantage of unrest in the Berber city of Aoudaghost to the west and captured it. After the Berbers were defeated, the Wagadou capital of Kumbi Saleh became the main center of trade in the western Sudan region. The Ghana Empire's power had risen to its greatest point.

Kumbi Saleh and the Rise of Islam

To learn about ancient Ghana, historians depend on the writings of Arabic scholars, many of whom lived in what was then Islamic Spain. Arab culture and science were at their height in the early Middle Ages. Arab princes hired scholars to interview traders and travelers and to write books about distant lands.

Arab Expansion

Islam came to Africa soon after the death of the prophet Muhammed in 632 CE. Unified by the new Muslim religion, Arab armies clashed with the Christian Byzantine Roman Empire, which controlled much of the Middle East and Egypt. Byzantine knights were no match for Arab horsemen in the desert and open grassland.

Arab armies under commander Amir ibn-al-'As invaded Byzantine-ruled Egypt in 639 CE. Within two years, his armies had spread Islam as far as the Nubian region south of Egypt. Pushing farther west, Arab armies found stronger resistance from the native Berber peoples of North Africa but finally conquered Morocco in 682 CE.

The Berber-speaking people living in Morocco, whom the Arabs had conquered, knew about a kingdom south of the

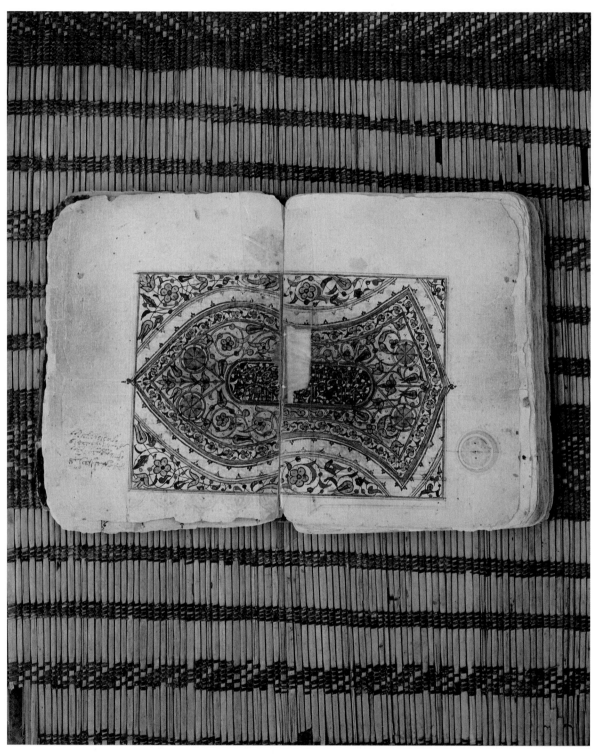

The kings of ancient Ghana valued Islamic scholars for their ability to keep detailed written records. This Islamic manuscript from the region depicts the sandal of the prophet Muhammed.

Sahara Desert that was rich in gold. The Arabs decided to split their army in two and attack both that kingdom and Spain.

The victorious Arab armies invaded Europe by crossing the Strait of Gibraltar and conquering Spain in 712 CE. Muslim Spain endured until the fall of Grenada in 1491.

Clash of Empires

The first Arab migration south into the fabled land of gold—the empire of Wagadou—was not very successful. The Arabs were surprised to find a powerful and organized army defending the region. They decided that it was better to trade with Wagadou than to fight its powerful armies. Many of the Bani Hassan Arab tribes that had formed the army took Berber wives and settled in the hills of Morocco, producing a new culture. They spoke a dialect of Arabic called Hassaniya and eventually became known as the Moors.

Soon Arab goods, ideas, Muslim religious beliefs, and scholars traveled to the empire of Wagadou. Because the Arabs brought a system of writing with them into Africa, their accounts, written in the Arabic language, are the earliest written descriptions of the empire.

The Arab Chronicles

Abjullah Abu-Ubaid al-Bakri was an Arab author and geographer who lived in Cordoba, Spain, during the eleventh century. In 1067, he wrote about the Empire of Ghana and its people and customs in *The Book of Routes and Realms*. Although he did not travel to the area himself, he talked to Arab merchants

THE BERBER PEOPLE

The Berber people play an important role in the history of the Sahara and of the Empire of Ghana. They call themselves *imazighen,* which means "free people." Berbers have lived in North Africa since ancient times and originally dwelled between the Nile River and the Atlantic Ocean. They speak a language, Tamazight, that is not related to Arabic or to any other African or European languages. Berber identity remains strong to this day in Morocco and Algeria. Berbers created the Almoravid dynasty in the eleventh century, which would eventually overrun Ghana.

The Tuareg are one of the most unique of the many Berber cultures. The Tuareg inhabit the Sahara Desert. Before the introduction of motor vehicles, they lived by leading the camel caravans that moved along the trans-Saharan trade routes. Tuaregs transported trade goods, food, and locally mined salt across the desert, stopping at oases along the way to eat and drink water.

Tuareg men are famous for the custom of wearing deep blue turbans and veils that cover their faces. Their name for themselves is *Kel Tagelmust,* or "people of the veil." The veil provides protection from Sahara sand and dust and is removed only in the company of close family. The veil is made blue by pounding indigo dye into the cloth, which often stains their skin blue as well, which earned them the label "blue men of the desert."

The Tuareg people are the masters of the Sahara, and their camel caravans still cross the desert sands to this day.

who did and wrote about what they told him. He also knew a great deal about the empire because Muslims from North Africa had invaded thirteen years before, in 1054, and had captured the important trading city of Aoudaghost.

Based on his conversations with eyewitnesses who had traveled and traded with the Ghana Empire, al-Bakri described a large city of thirty thousand people, which he called "Al-Ghaba." Today, we know this city as Kumbi Saleh. Unfortunately, al-Bakri left no information as to where the city was located, and for centuries it was truly a lost city.

As was common in Africa, the "city" was actually two separate cities, located about 6 miles (9.7 kilometers) apart. The Soninke lived in one city, and foreign traders lived in the other. The city inhabited by foreigners (mostly Muslim merchants and scholars) had large, rectangular stone houses—a North African influence. Like homes in the Soninke city, houses in the Muslim city were built along narrow streets that led to a wide avenue, where the outdoor market was located. The foreigners' city also had twelve mosques, where the Muslims worshipped. In fact, the Empire of Ghana became wealthy because of its contacts with and acceptance of Muslim traders and scholars.

El-Ghaba

The Wagadou emperor lived in the Soninke city. Al-Bakri described this part of Al-Ghaba as a walled fortress. The circular houses had clay walls and large, wooden beams that supported thatched, dome-shaped roofs. The homes of wealthy people were made of stone and wood. The largest and most elaborate house was the emperor's palace.

The Wagadou emperor held court in this impressive palace, which was luxuriously decorated with paintings, sculptures, and gold. The king himself was splendidly dressed. At the height of the Ghana Empire's power, he was the only Soninke allowed to wear imported and tailored clothing. Everyone else living in Al-Ghaba wore simpler cotton, silk, or brocade cloth draped around their bodies.

The Rediscovery of Kumbi Saleh

After the fall of the Empire of Ghana, the royal city of Kumbi Saleh rapidly declined in importance, as the focus of trade shifted to settlements along the Niger River to the southeast. Newer states, such as the empires of Mali and Songhay, however, would draw much of their power and fame from ancestral connections to the ruling families of the empire. Griots—singers of ballads—kept the epics of Ghana alive in their songs, and scholars skilled in Arabic writing made note of the fame of the Ghana Empire. A written history of the Songhay Empire—the *Tarikh al-Fattash*, written by Mahmud Kati in the seventeenth century—mentions the city of Kumbi Saleh by name.

During the early nineteenth century, the Sahel region was the scene of a religious war led by nomadic Fulani herdsmen, who wished to reform Islamic practice to a more strict form. In a practice that would sadly be repeated throughout history, the nomads ordered all books and libraries burned, and the *Tarikh al-Fattash* was thought to have been lost forever. But in

Some archaeologists believe today's Kumbi Saleh was once the capital city of the Ghana Empire, but it is hard to know for sure. The mud and straw construction of Sahel houses means that only dust remains once a town is abandoned.

1896, a copy was found and a translation into French was made in 1911. Finally, scientists had clues as to the location of Kumbi Saleh.

The ruins of Kumbi Saleh are found in today's nation of Mauritania, on a dry plain that gives little clue to the grand city that was once the magnet of an international trade network. Archaeologists—scientists who study how people lived in the past—began digging up the remains of the city soon after its discovery in 1914. Some scientists are still not convinced that this dusty ruin in the Sahel wasteland is the real Kumbi Saleh of the Ghana kings. However, in 1977, an expedition found small glass weights that had been used by gold traders to balance their gold scales. Based on evidence like this, archaeologists continue to search for more clues to the elusive Empire of Ghana.

CHAPTER FOUR

Religion and Power

The Empire of Ghana provided the first meeting place for Islam and the traditional belief systems of West Africa. The result was an approach to Islam that became particularly African in practice. The Islamic influence on the Ghana Empire shapes the religious and political situation of West Africa and the Sahel region to this very day.

The traditional religion of the Soninke was described by the Spanish Arabic historian al-Bakri, gathered from tales told by Muslim traders and travelers. Like many medieval historians, al-Bakri was especially interested in descriptions of the king and his court and their main city, which he called Al-Ghaba.

The name Al-Ghaba means "the forest." It referred to a sacred grove of bushes within the Soninke part of the city. The grove contained the royal tombs and statues of past kings. The entire city was considered sacred because it was both the royal center and the spiritual center of the empire.

The Power of Ancestors

According to al-Bakri, the Soninke inhabitants of Al-Ghaba were not Muslim, and the city had only one mosque, which was built for visiting Muslim dignitaries. In the later years of the Empire of Ghana, increasing numbers of people converted

The distant cities of West Africa—and their gold mines—caught the imaginations of the early Arab geographers of Islamic Spain.

to Islam. Many of the emperor's ministers became Muslim. The ruling Soninke people, however, remained non-Muslim. They followed a religion that was centered on their ancestors.

The ancestors, especially the royal ancestors, were thought to be very powerful. Their power came from their close connections to the spirit world and the world of the living. The Soninke people believed that the ancestors could speak the languages of both worlds and that they could speak to the spirits on behalf of their descendants. Therefore, if the living took care of their ancestors, the ancestors would take care of their descendants.

The Holy Snake

The Soninke religion was also based on the legend of a great and powerful black snake named Wagadou-Bida. The holy snake was believed to live in a cave inside the sacred grove and was the guardian spirit of the royal clan. Because the snake guarded the king's soul, and the king was considered the divine ruler and protector of the empire and its people, Wagadou-Bida was seen as the guardian of the empire. This is one explanation of why the Soninke people called themselves the people of Wagadou. The other explanation is that the name is related to the word *wago*, which is the name of the Soninke ruling class.

Royal Burial

Al-Bakri mentioned royal tombs in the sacred forest grove. He wrote that the grove, the snake, and the graves of the ancestral kings were guarded by priests, who would not allow anyone into the grove. The kings themselves entered the grove only twice: when they were crowned and when they died. Kings, and perhaps their sisters and mothers, were buried in royal tombs inside the grove. The tombs were outfitted with everything the kings might want or need in the next life, the life after death. Food, clothing, jewelry, weapons, and even furniture were all buried in the tomb with the deceased rulers. Some of the king's servants were also buried with him in the royal tomb. In this way, it was believed, the servants could continue to serve their king throughout eternity.

MODERN-DAY SLAVERY

As shocking as it may seem, slavery is very much alive in the region that was once home to the Empire of Ghana. While abolished in Mauritania only in 1981, slavery is still widespread. According to SOS Slaves, more than five hundred thousand people—about 18 percent of the population—are enslaved. In Mali, the French colonial powers abolished slavery in 1905, but it still exists in rural communities. Elsewhere in Africa, slavery continues to be a problem in the Sahel states of Niger, Chad, and Sudan. International organizations, such as the United Nations and Antislavery International, are working to end slavery and help those affected by this terrible practice.

While slavery is not legal in Mauritania, people may be born into a slave class, and many, such as these herdsmen, are still trapped in exploitative systems.

These three key religious beliefs—ancestor worship, a creation myth centered upon a mythical guardian snake, and the maintenance of sacred forests—became widespread among West African cultures over a large geographic area. Perhaps these beliefs show the strong influence of the Ghana Empire. As Islam spread among the African peoples south of the Sahara, it would often find strong opposition among believers in the traditional faiths.

An Empire Adorned

The Empire of Ghana's fabled wealth dazzled writers like al-Bakri. He wrote that the king and members of his court wore elegant gold jewelry and gold clothing. Gold was also used for the royal emblems and ornaments and for drums, shields, and swords. The Wagadou kings used their great wealth to impress visitors, showing them how rich and powerful the empire was.

The great riches of the Ghana Empire included many arts and a flourishing culture. Kumbi Saleh's markets were filled with exotic foods, arts, and merchandise from all over Africa and beyond. All of these goods were paid for with gold dust.

Slavery in the Sahel

Kumbi Saleh's market was also a source of slaves. Northern merchants bought slaves, whom the Soninke had captured from smaller and weaker peoples to the south, and took them north, where there was a steady demand for them. These African slaves might be sold to slave markets on the shores of the Mediterranean Sea, but most were settled on farms across

North Africa, where they were called *haratin*. The young men were often taken away for military service; the sultan of Morocco maintained a special elite unit of his army made up of African slaves called the Black Guard, which existed as recently as 1956. To this day, African communities in Morocco are called Gnawa—a word derived from the name "Ghana." Gnawa music has become a popular style of Moroccan music. It is played on percussion instruments and uses a banjo-like stringed instrument called a *guimbri* that shows direct African influence.

Gnawa music has become one of the most popular styles in Moroccan music. The box-like *guimbri* is similar to the American banjo: both share a common African ancestry.

Slavery was widespread in West Africa and the Arabic Maghreb regions of North Africa. Slaves were "owned" by a regional ruler and made to work on farms or in building projects. As Africans adopted the Arabic language and Muslim religion, many became powerful and rich themselves, which led some to become slave owners as well.

An Uneasy Balance

Modern archaeologists digging in the remains of Kumbi Saleh have found a great deal of evidence pointing to the wealth of the empire but little solid gold. They have discovered many pottery fragments, glass counterweights for gold, metal weapons, knives, farming tools, nails, and even stones painted with verses from the Koran, the Islamic holy book.

The abundance of gold attracted not only traders from the north but also their ideas. The majority of these traders were Berbers who had themselves only recently converted to the Muslim religion. Muslim merchants residing in the double city of Al-Ghaba often married local women, and many Africans found it to their advantage to adopt Islam as their religion. The Soninke of the royal clan, however, did not convert, maintaining their status as "living gods" in the traditional religious view. Yet this peaceful balance could not last forever.

Tensions between the Berber converts to Islam and their Arabic leaders in Morocco and Spain led many Berbers to question the purity of their Arab leadership's religious outlooks. The Berbers expanded southward into the desert and established a trading city at Aoudaghost, just to the north of the kingdom of

Ghana. At some time, Ghana conquered Aoudaghost, and the king went to live there with his court.

Around 1030 CE, War Jabi, the king of Tekrur, a kingdom of the Serer people to the west of Ghana along the Atlantic coast, became the first African king to convert to Islam. Many of the Serer people refused to give up their traditional religion. War broke out in Tekrur, and the Serer pushed War Jabi and his Muslim allies north to areas controlled by the Berbers. The Berbers and their new Serer allies soon moved to recapture Aoudaghost.

CHAPTER FIVE

The Fall of Kumbi Saleh

By 1000 CE, as Europe was emerging from the Dark Ages, the Islamic state—known as the Caliphate—spread from Central Asia in the east to Aoudaghost and Tekrur in the western Sahel. The kingdom of Ghana was about to face an invasion of Muslims from the north. This struggle would mark the final chapter of the Ghana Empire.

A Legend of the Fall

The Soninke people told a legend about Wagadou-Bida—the great black snake that lived in the sacred grove of Kumbi Saleh—that attempted to explain the fall of the Empire of Ghana. Like many legends, it does not try to argue historical fact but works to give a sense of meaning to a major historical event. The legend has been passed down as follows.

In the beginning, before the Wagadou kingdom developed into the mighty Empire of Ghana and before the Soninke's first ancestor, Dinga, arrived, Bida lived in the western Sudan. After Dinga and his family settled in the region, one of Dinga's sons, Dyabe, made a deal with the snake. Dyabe agreed that once a year, the most beautiful young woman in the society would be sacrificed to Bida. In return, Bida allowed Dyabe and his Soninke

Both the traditional stories of the Soninke and modern scientists agree that the fall of Kumbi Saleh may have been caused by climate change.

descendants to build a great city, which became known as Kumbi Saleh. But the legend tells us that one year a young warrior loved the young woman who was about to be sacrificed. He loved her so much that he decided to kill Bida to save her life.

The warrior, whose name was Amadou Sefedokote, hid in the sacred grove. When Bida came out of his cave, Amadou cut off its head. The sacred snake was powerful, however. Each time Amadou cut off its head, a new one grew in its place. It was not until the seventh head was cut that the snake finally

THE ALMORAVIDS

Additional information about why the Ghana Empire collapsed comes from historical texts. Arab writers tell us that the ancient kingdom of the Soninke fell because of economic and political problems. After the Empire of Ghana reached its greatest power in the eleventh century, competition with its neighbors for control of trade weakened its power.

The empire finally fell to the Almoravids, a religious group of Berber nomads. Under the leadership of their founder, Abdallah Ibn Yasin, the Almoravids strictly followed the teachings of the Koran.

The Almoravid movement began around 1040 CE, when a Muslim Berber leader, Yahya ibn Ibrahim, made the hajj. This is a pilgrimage to the holy city of Mecca (located in what is today Saudi Arabia) that is required of all devout Muslims. On his return home, he passed through Egypt, then ruled by the Fatimid dynasty. The Fatimids were Shia Muslims, a sect that many orthodox conservative Sunni Muslims considered to be heretics—believers in a wrong teaching. Yahya appointed a young Moroccan Berber, Ibn Yasin, to preach a more pure form of Sunni Islam to the Berber tribes in Morocco.

Ibn Yasin preached that it was not enough to spread the word of Islam but that one also had to actively and violently oppose those who did not believe in it. He forbade the drinking of wine, the playing of music, and the collection of taxes by non-Muslims. Almoravids also opposed many of the liberal aspects of Islam, and they believed that men as well as women should veil their faces. From this came the practice of men wearing a turban and veil, which continues among the desert-dwelling Tuareg of the Sahara to this day.

Many of the Sanhaja Berber tribes, who had lost their lands and their city of Aoudaghost to the Ghana Empire, joined in Ibn Yasin's new religious movement. Calling themselves the Al-Murabitin, or "those who are bound to fight," the Almoravids attacked Aoudaghost in 1055, securing the valuable Sahara Desert trade route.

died. The woman, whose name was Sia, was saved. But because Dyabe's promise had been broken, terrible things began to happen to the Soninke.

Each head that Amadou cut off is said to have flown through the air. The site where each head landed suddenly became rich with gold. This meant that the Soninke no longer had sole control over the gold market, and they lost the power that went with their control.

In addition, after the snake died, a terrible drought fell upon the land. The drought lasted seven years. The farmers' crops died, and the Soninke had little to eat or drink. The great cities like Kumbi Saleh were abandoned.

A Victim of Global Warming?

This legend may give us a clue as to what really brought about the end of the powerful Empire of Ghana. Perhaps a terrible drought did indeed weaken the empire.

Scientists today can look into the weather patterns of the past by drilling for ice cores in the Arctic and by examining the growth rings on ancient trees. Scientists tell us that a period of global warming, called the Medieval Warm Period, occurred between 950 and 1250 CE, causing the warmest weather Earth had seen for two thousand years. During this time, the Northern Hemisphere was so warm that the Vikings were able to settle and farm in Arctic Greenland. The effect in Africa was that the arid Sahara began to spread into the Sahel, drying out areas that were once able to sustain the farming and livestock necessary to the Ghana Empire. After 1250, the climate returned to normal, allowing people to return to farming in the Sahel. Unfortunately, the freezing climate in the northern seas led to the disappearance of the Vikings in Greenland!

The Conquest of Ghana

Although the Wagadou kings had allowed religious freedom within their kingdom—including the Islamic faith—the Almoravids would not tolerate non-Muslim beliefs. They regarded as offensive the Soninke belief in many gods and that the king was divine. These Soninke beliefs violated the rule in the Koran against worshipping gods other than Allah. After the reconquest of Aoudaghost in 1055, the Serer royal clan led by War Jabi invited the Almoravids to attack the peoples to the

Islam transformed society in West Africa and brought it into closer contact with the Mediterranean world.

south who had resisted the religion of Islam: the Soninke, Fulani, Wolof, and Mandinka.

In 1055, Ibn Yasin's successor, Abu Bakr, led the Almoravid armies and captured the city of Aoudaghost. Then, in 1070, they invaded the territory of the original Wagadou kingdom. The Almoravids finally defeated the empire's armies and conquered Kumbi Saleh in 1076.

Where were the famed armies of Ghana? Perhaps by this time they had become merely a legend of the empire's former greatness. Perhaps climate change hastened the decline of Kumbi Saleh. The climate in 1076 was warming, and the Sahara Desert was spreading into the region where Kumbi Saleh stood. Soon the focus of the trade routes shifted farther south, along the Niger River. If Kumbi Saleh was doomed to become desert, there was little to tie the Soninke farmers to it.

The Almoravids did not remain in control of Ghana for very long. They began to focus their attention on the state of Islam in Muslim Spain. In 1086, the Almoravid leader Yusuf ibn Tashfin crossed the Strait of Gibraltar into Spain. The Almoravid army—numbering over fifteen thousand men, including over eight thousand African troops—defeated the Christian knights of King Alonzo IV of Castile. Spain was now safely a part of the Islamic world. Almoravid Berbers became known as the Moors, and the era of Muslim rule in western Europe came to be known as Moorish Spain.

CHAPTER SIX

Decline and Rebirth

No written account exists of the actual fall of the Empire of Ghana. We do know that the Almoravids defeated Ghana and that the Soninke people began to adopt the Islamic religion soon after. Perhaps we cannot really speak of the Ghana Empire as having "fallen." Like other empires, such as Rome, it endured through a period of change and eventually found itself much different from what it had been at Kumbi Saleh.

A New Kingdom

It is quite likely that Muslim counselors in the court of the last pagan king, Tunka-Manin, took advantage of the Almoravid threat to topple the king. They installed their own Muslim ruler, Kema Magha, who began to promote Islam within the kingdom. When the Arab historian Al-Idrisi wrote about Ghana in 1154, he mentioned that it was thoroughly Muslim by that time.

When the non-Muslims of the empire began to revolt against Muslim reforms, members of the Cissé family of Kema Magha fled. They went eastward, down the Niger River to the city of Gao, where Islam had taken stronger hold among the Sosso, a

GRIOTS AND THEIR MUSIC

Oral history tells us that when Sundiata Keita began his struggle against the Sosso, his father presented him with a griot named Balla Fasseke Kouyate to advise him on how to rule properly. From that day on, the Kouyate family have served the rulers of Mali and every subsequent government in the Sahel as griots. Sundiata Keita's final request to his people at his death was to honor the griots!

Griots, known as *jali* in Mandinka and *jaaré* in Soninke, are singers of epic ballads. They serve as living libraries of history, preserving the histories of the great families of the Sahel empires going as far back as the Empire of Ghana. Griots are born into special families of musicians who live by singing the praises and histories of rich and elite families. Griot families are considered part of a lower social caste. They are also feared because of their dedication to singing only the truth.

The music of the griots is played on a variety of instruments. During the era of the Ghana Empire, Soninke griots preferred to play the *ngoni*, a small three-string instrument. It may be the ancestor of the banjo, which West African slaves brought to America more than three hundred years ago. Today, many griots also use the modern guitar. The *balafon* is a wooden xylophone that uses

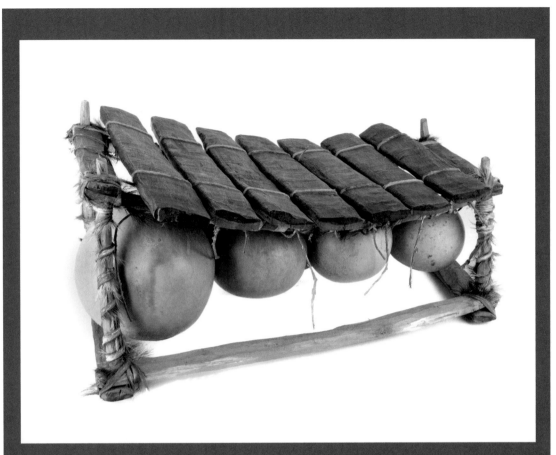

The *balafon* is one of the instruments played by the Kouyate family of griots, who can trace their lineage as far back as the Empire of Ghana.

gourds to produce a loud, booming sound. The *kora* is probably the most widespread instrument among griot musicians. It is a twenty-one-string harp constructed from a large gourd, animal skin, and strings (now made from nylon fishing line). Producing delicate, melodic music, the kora has become an international hit in the hands of world-famous griot musicians.

people related to the Soninke. Gao then grew to become a new center of Cissé power.

The Sosso of Gao, led by Diara Kante, took Kumbi Saleh for themselves in 1180, and they began wars against the Mandinka people along the Niger. During these wars, one family of the Keita clan fled to Wagadou for protection against a revengeful king. There, they had a son, Sundiata Keita, who could not walk until he was seven years old. Thus, he was not seen as a threat. But Sundiata finally stood up at the age of seven to avenge an insult to his mother. He went on to become a great warrior king who united the Mandinka against the Sosso and founded the kingdom of Mali in 1235. The legend of Sundiata Keita should be familiar: it provided the background story for the Disney film *The Lion King*.

The Sahel Today

The history of Ghana gradually blends into the history of later Sahel

The epic lessons of the empires of Ghana, Mali, and Songhay continue to inspire today's generation of African children.

kingdoms—first Mali and later Songhay. The trade in gold and slaves continued as before. The Mali and Songhay kingdoms grew in wealth until they were, in turn, invaded and subdued, only for the cycle to begin again under a new ruler or clan of nomads. Eventually, Europeans came to rule the kingdoms of the western Sudan region as French or English colonies. However, they, too, were swept into the sands of history. Today, the nations of Mali, Mauritania, Niger, and Burkina Faso represent the heritage of the Empire of Ghana, while the Republic of Ghana proudly bears its name.

The violence that tore at the Ghana Empire disrupts the region today. Tension between settled Africans and nomadic

The never-ending struggle between the rivers and the desert will always define life in the shadow of the Empire of Ghana.

Tuaregs continues. In recent times, Tuaregs have fought for self-rule in both Mauritania and Mali.

In Mali, the terrorist group Ansar Dine seeks to impose strict Islamic law and is said to have ties to terrorist group Al-Qaeda. After taking over the city of Timbuktu in 2012, militants from Ansar Dine tried to destroy the ancient Sidi Yahya Mosque, housing the shrines of local Sufi Muslim saints. They also attempted to destroy the libraries of the ancient religious schools, housing hundreds of historically important scrolls and books. These materials hold the key to knowledge about past kingdoms such as Ghana. When French-led forces liberated Timbuktu a few months later, it was found that local families had hidden most of these precious books.

The relationships in the Sahel and Sahara today—between nomads and farmers, desert and town dwellers—are still troubled by religious rivalry and tribal loyalties. On the shores of this great sea of sand, empires come and empires go. But their stories—beginning with Ghana and the great kings of Wagadou—remain alive in the melodies of the griots' harps, the pages of ancient books, and the ever-shifting sands of the desert.

TIMELINE

c. 250 Ancient Ghana is possibly established by Soninke-speaking peoples.

c. 570 The prophet Muhammed is born.

c. 680 Arabs reach Morocco in northwest Africa.

c. 712 Arabs invade Spain.

c. 750 Ancient Ghana begins to flourish.

c. 950 The Medieval Warm Period begins, causing the climate to dry out the Sahara Desert.

c. 990 Ancient Ghana captures Aoudaghost.

1030 War Jabi, king of neighboring Tekrur, converts to Islam.

1054 Abu Bakr leads the Almoravid armies to capture Aoudaghost.

1066 William the Conqueror invades England.

1067 Abjullah Abu-Ubaid al-Bakri, Arab author and geographer from Cordoba, Spain, writes about ancient Ghana.

1070 Almoravid armies invade Wagadou.

1076 Almoravids defeat the Wagadou armies and conquer Kumbi Saleh.

1180 Sosso rulers from Gao conquer Kumbi Saleh and oppress non-Muslim Mandinka peoples.

1235 Sundiata Keita defeats the Sosso king Soumare Cissé and establishes the kingdom of Mali.

1250 Wagadou joins the empire of Mali.

1350 Mali conquers Gao.

1450–1600 The empire of Songhay flourishes.

1914 The ruins of Kumbi Saleh are found by archaeologists.

GLOSSARY

Almoravids Nomadic Berber Muslims, members of an extremely pious religious sect.

Aoudaghost An important trading city captured by the Ghanaian kingdom in 990 CE and then by the Almoravids in 1054 CE.

brocade A textile whose decoration is made by "floating" some of the woven threads across the top of the fabric, creating a smooth pattern.

caravan A string of pack animals, such as camels or horses, that carries people and goods across long distances.

clan A group of families that have all descended from a single ancestor.

dialect A variety of a language that is different and distinct but still understandable.

feudal system A European political system under which the people work for and pay taxes to an overlord, who owns the land on which they work.

griot A professional oral historian among the Mandinka, Wolof, and other West African peoples who studies, recounts, and keeps alive history through song.

hajj The religious pilgrimage, or visit, to the holy city of Mecca that every Muslim is required to do in his or her life, if he or she is able.

heretic One who holds beliefs that are opposed to accepted beliefs.

Koran The holy book of Islam.

matrilineal Relating to a system of descent in which power and identity are passed down through the mother.

Muslim One who follows the religion of Islam.

oasis A place in a desert that has water fed by underground springs.

petroglyph A painting or etching carved in stone cliffs.

regalia The objects, symbols, and decorations worn or displayed to symbolize royalty.

Sahel The grassland region south of the Sahara Desert.

sedentary Settled down in one place.

Sharia The moral code and religious law of Islam.

tribute Payment made to a ruler in the form of taxes or goods.

FOR MORE INFORMATION

African Studies Association (ASA)
Rutgers University—Livingston Campus
54 Joyce Kilmer Avenue
Piscataway, NJ 08854
(848) 445-8173
Web site: http://www.africanstudies.org
Established in 1957, the ASA is the largest organization
    devoted to enhancing the exchange of information
    about Africa. It encourages the production and dissemi-
    nation of knowledge about Africa, past and present.

African Studies Center at Boston University
232 Bay State Road
Boston, MA 02215
(617) 353-3673
Web site: http://www.bu.edu/africa
The African Studies Center at Boston University is one of
    the oldest and largest research centers for African stud-
    ies in the United States. It has an extensive Web site
    featuring resources for students and teachers.

Anti-Slavery International
Thomas Clarkson House
The Stableyard
Broomgrove Road
London SW9 9TL
United Kingdom
Web site: http://www.antislavery.org

Anti-Slavery International works at local, national, and international levels to eliminate all forms of slavery around the world. Nations whose land was once included in the kingdom of Ghana, such as Mali, Mauritania, and Niger, struggle with ongoing slavery.

Embassy of Mali in the United States
2130 R Street NW
Washington, DC 20008
(202) 332-2249
Web site: http://www.maliembassy.us
The Embassy of Mali provides diplomatic representation, as well as cultural information, about the modern African nation of Mali, which is located at the heart of the region in which the Empire of Ghana flourished.

Institute of African Studies
Carleton University
228 Paterson Hall
1125 Colonel By Drive
Ottawa, ON K1S 5B6
Canada
(613) 520-2600, ext. 2220
Web site: http://www2.carleton.ca/africanstudies
Carleton is the only Canadian university to have a stand-alone institute of African studies that offers a degree program. The program focuses on history, modern African issues and culture, and the African diaspora and the consequences of transatlantic slavery.

Sahara Conservation Fund
Rue des Tigneuses 2
1148 L'Isle
Switzerland
Web site: http://www.saharaconservation.org
The mission of the Sahara Conservation Fund is to conserve
the wildlife, habitat, and other natural resources of the
Sahara and its surrounding Sahelian grasslands. Its vision
is of a Sahara that supports all of its inhabitants.

Web Sites

Due to the changing nature of Internet links, Rosen
Publishing has developed an online list of Web sites related
to the subject of this book. This site is updated regularly.
Please use this link to access the list:

http://www.rosenlinks.com/EAC/Ghana

FOR FURTHER READING

Austen, Ralph A. *Trans-Saharan Africa in World History*. New York, NY: Oxford University Press, 2010.

Conrad, David C. *Empires of Medieval West Africa: Ghana, Mali, and Songhay* (Great Empires of the Past). Rev. ed. New York, NY: Chelsea House, 2010.

Gearon, Eamonn. *The Sahara: A Cultural History*. New York, NY: Oxford University Press, 2011.

Green, Jen. *West African Myths* (Myths from Around the World). New York, NY: Gareth Stevens Publishing, 2010.

Heinrichs, Ann. *The Sahara* (Nature's Wonders). New York, NY: Marshall Cavendish Benchmark, 2009.

Klobuchar, Lisa. *Africans of the Ghana, Mali, Songhai Empires* (Early Peoples). Chicago, IL: World Book, 2009.

Middleton, John, and Joseph Calder Miller. *New Encyclopedia of Africa*. Detroit, MI: Thomson/Gale, 2008.

Pouwels, Randall Lee. *The African and Middle Eastern World, 600–1500*. New York, NY: Oxford University Press, 2005.

Seligman, Thomas K., ed. *Art of Being Tuareg: Sahara Nomads in a Modern World*. Los Angeles, CA: UCLA Fowler Museum, 2006.

Sherrow, Victoria, and James R. Denbow. *Ancient Africa: Archaeology Unlocks the Secrets of Africa's Past* (National Geographic Investigates). Washington, DC: National Geographic Society, 2007.

Wise, Christopher, and Mahmud Kati. *Tarikh al-Fattash: The Timbuktu Chronicles 1493–1599*. Trenton, NJ: African World Press, 2012.

INDEX

About the Author

Robert Z. Cohen was born in New York City and studied cultural anthropology with a special concentration in African studies at Boston University in Boston, Massachusetts. There, he studied several African languages, including Yoruba, Ewe, and Zulu, as well as Haitian Creole. He has traveled around the Caribbean researching memories of African languages. Cohen moved to Budapest, Hungary, to research the language and music of the Romani (Gypsy) people. He works as a journalist and travel guide writer, and he leads his own klezmer band on tours around Europe and North America.

Photo Credits